THE CRITICS RAVE!

"This book is an insult."
—Anonymous, Esq.

"Most of the jokes really are not funny and are in poor taste."
—Peter L. Malkin
Attorney at Law

"[This book] perpetuates unfair stereotypes. So hire a joke writer the next time you are in trouble."
—John J. Grillos, Esq.

SKID MARKS

common jokes about lawyers

edited by Michael Rafferty

SHELTER PUBLICATIONS, INC.
P.O. BOX 279, BOLINAS, CALIF. 94924

Copyright © 1988 by Shelter Publications, Inc.

Distributed in the United States by
TEN SPEED PRESS
P.O. Box 7123
Berkeley, California 94707

**Library of Congress
Cataloging in Publication Data**

Skid marks.

    Includes index.
    1. Law -- Humor. I. Rafferty, Michael, 1940
PN6231.L4S45 1988   818'.5402'08   88-11374
ISBN 0—936070—08—0
ISBN 0—89815—283—6 (Ten Speed Press)

Additional copies of this book may be
purchased at your favorite bookstore or
by sending $3.95 per book plus shipping
charges of $1.50 1st book, 50 cents each
additional book to:

**Shelter Publications, Inc.
P.O. Box 279
Bolinas, CA 94924**

3 4 5 6 7 8 9 - 95 94 93 92 90

The legal profession has been much abused; but whether abused most by an ignorant public or its own unworthy members, would perhaps be difficult to say. Law and justice are so great, so grand, so deep and broad and divine, that men cannot easily understand them or appreciate their dignity.

Science of Self, 1892

"And if I laugh at any mortal thing,
'Tis that I may not weep."
                    —Lord Byron

What is the difference between a dead skunk and a dead lawyer in the middle of the road?

There are skid marks
in front of the skunk.

A man went to see a lawyer and asked what his least expensive fee was. The lawyer replied, "$50 for three questions."

Stunned, the man asked, "Isn't that a lot of money for three questions?"

"Yes, the lawyer said. "What is your final question?"

What's black and brown and
looks good on a lawyer?

A doberman.

What do you call 2,000 attorneys chained together at the bottom of the sea?

A good beginning.

A well-known attorney found himself at heaven's gates confronting St. Peter. He protested that it was all a mistake: he was only 52 and far too young to be dead.

"That's strange", said St. Peter, "according to your time sheets, you're 89 years old."

THE L

ROBINSONS. BRISTOL

419

It seemed that the son of a Spanish lawyer graduated from college and was considering the future. He went to his father, who had a very large office, and asked if he might be given a desk in a corner where he could observe his father's activities. He could be introduced to the clients as a clerk. This way, he could decide whether or not to become a lawyer. His father thought this a splendid idea, and the arrangement was set up immediately.

On the son's first day at work, the first client in the morning was a rough-hewn man with calloused hands, in workman's attire, who began the conversation as follows:

"Mr. Lawyer, I work for some people named Gonzales who have a ranch on the east side of town. For many years I have tended their crops and animals, including some cows. I have raised the cows, tended them, fed them, and it has always been my understanding and belief that I was the owner of the cows. Mr. Gonzales died and his son has inherited the farm, and he believes that since the cows were raised on his ranch and fed on his hay, the cows are his. In short, we have a dispute as to the ownership of the cows."

The lawyer said, "I have heard enough. I will take your case. DON'T WORRY ABOUT THE COWS!"

After the tenant farmer left, the next client came in. A young, well-dressed man, clearly a member of the landed class. "My name is Gonzales. I own a farm on the east side of the town," he said. "For many years, a tenant farmer has worked for my family tending the crops and animals, including some cows. The cows have been raised on my land and fed on my hay, and I believe they belong to me, but the tenant farmer believes that since he raised them and cared for them, they are his. In short, we have a dispute over the ownership of the cows."

"I've heard enough. I'll take your case. DON'T WORRY ABOUT THE COWS!"

After the client left, the son came over to his father with a look of concern. "My father, I know nothing about the law, but it seems to me that we have a serious problem regarding these cows."

"DON'T WORRY ABOUT THE COWS!" said the lawyer. "The cows will be ours!"

Upon seeing an elderly lady for the drafting
of her will, the attorney charged her $100.
She gave him a $100 bill, not noticing that
stuck to it was a second $100 bill.
Immediately the ethical question arose in
the attorney's mind:

"Do I tell my partner?"

How can you tell if a lawyer is lying?

His lips are moving.

A lawyer had a jury trial in a very difficult business case. The client who had attended the trial was out of town at the time the jury came back with its decision. The decision was a complete victory for the lawyer and his client. The lawyer excitedly sent a telegram to the client, which read, simply:

"Justice has triumphed!"

The client, a realistic man, received the telegram and wired back:

"Appeal at once!"

A blind rabbit and a blind snake met one another in the woods, hit it off pretty well, and over a period of months met on a daily basis.

One day the snake said, "We've known one another for a long time now, and I just realized that I don't even know what you look like. Would you mind if I felt you?"

The rabbit said, "O.K., sure, fine," and let the snake coil around him.

"Goodness," said the snake, "you are soft and warm and furry, and you have big ears. Are you, by any chance, a rabbit?"

"Yes, I am," said the rabbit. "And you—you are cold and slimy and you have fangs and scales. Could it be that you are a lawyer?"

Why don't lawyers go to the beach?

The cats keep trying to bury them.

Standing around the grave of a departed friend are an anthropologist, a doctor, and a lawyer.

When the eulogies are over, the anthropologist suggests that they all put some money in the coffin, as is the practice of some ancient tribes he has been studying.

The anthropologist pulls out a $100 bill and deposits it lovingly in the coffin. Not to be outdone, the doctor also pulls out a $100 bill and deposits it in the coffin.

The lawyer writes a check for $300, puts it in the coffin, and removes the $200 cash.

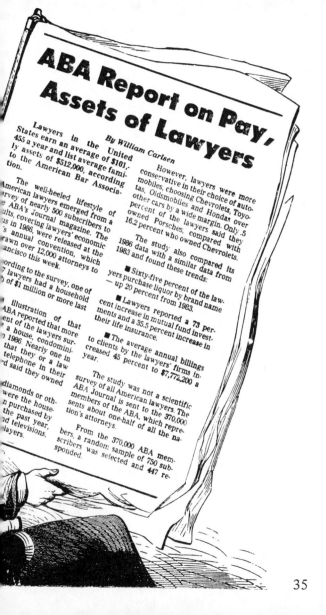

ABA Report on Pay, Assets of Lawyers

By William Carlsen

Lawyers in the United States earn an average of $101,455 a year and list average family assets of $512,000, according to the American Bar Association.

The well-heeled lifestyle of American lawyers emerged from a survey of nearly 500 subscribers to the ABA's Journal magazine. The results, covering lawyers' economic status in 1986, were released at the group's annual convention, which drew over 12,000 attorneys to San Francisco this week.

According to the survey, one of 7 lawyers had a household worth of $1 million or more last year.

In illustration of that wealth, the ABA reported that more than 83 percent of the lawyers surveyed own a house, condominium or co-op. In 1986, nearly one in five reported that they or a law firm had a telephone in their car, and one-third said they owned computers.

In addition to diamonds or other jewelry, which were the household luxuries most often purchased by respondents in the past year, 91.6 percent owned televisions, and 60 percent owned compact disc players.

However, lawyers were more conservative in their choice of automobiles, choosing Chevrolets, Toyotas, Oldsmobiles and Hondas over other cars by a wide margin. Only .5 percent of the lawyers said they owned Porsches, compared with 16.2 percent who owned Chevrolets.

The study also compared its 1986 data with a similar data from 1983 and found these trends:

■ Sixty-five percent of the lawyers purchase liquor by brand name — up 20 percent from 1983.

■ Lawyers reported a 73 percent increase in mutual fund investments and a 35.5 percent increase in their life insurance.

■ The average annual billings to clients by the lawyers' firms increased 45 percent to $7,772,200 a year.

The study was not a scientific survey of all American lawyers. The ABA Journal is sent to the 370,000 members of the ABA, which represents about one-half of all the nation's attorneys.

From the 370,000 ABA members, a random sample of 750 subscribers was selected and 447 responded.

Yuppie lawyers don't cry—they just Saab.

A priest, a doctor and a lawyer are killed in a bus crash and all arrive at heaven together. The priest is just awed. Heaven is really heavenly. The streets are lined with mansions and paved with gold.

St. Peter puts his arm around the priest and says, "Michael, it's wonderful to have another priest here. Come, I'll show you your new home."

Nestled on a grassy knoll is a charming cottage. Roses grow over the doorway and birds sing in the surrounding trees. "It's everything I ever wanted, says the priest. May I continue on with you to see where my friends are going to live?"

"Certainly," says St. Peter. The sun is shining, flowers are blooming and the air is fresh and clean. As they progress, the lawns and gardens get more magnificent and the houses more palatial.

Stopping before a 40-room mansion, St. Peter says, "Dr. Bob, you have spent your life caring for your fellow man and this home, with 12 bathrooms, 15 fireplaces and a staff of 20 is yours for eternity." You need never work again."

"Thank you," says Dr. Bob. "I am a little tired after my life's work. I think I'll take a short nap."

St. Peter, the lawyer, and the priest walk on, and the neighborhood continues to improve. Rounding a bend, they see a magnificent mansion on a knoll, surrounded by a garden of blooming flowers. The priest wonders if the mansion might be the home of one of the saints, or even of the Lord Himself.

As they mount the marble stairs to the front door, St. Peter says to the lawyer, "Son, this is your eternal home."

The attorney nods, and without saying a word, opens the door. The priest catches a glimpse of a hallway paved with lapis lazuli and gold, and as the lawyer disappears inside, St. Peter shouts after him, "If you want anything, just pick up the red phone. It's connected to my office. And if, for any reason, I'm unable to satisfy your needs, use the white phone. It's a direct line to God."

As they walk away, the priest is lost in thought.

"Do you mind if I ask a question," he says.

"Go right ahead," replies St. Peter.

"Well, I don't mean to complain," says the priest, "but I'd like to know why that lawyer deserves more of a reward than Dr. Bob or myself."

"That's easy," says St. Peter, "We get a lot of priests, and a few doctors, but that man was our first lawyer."

God and the devil were having a business discussion.

The Lord said, "I'm thinking of having some repair work done on the pearly gates, and I think you should pay half."

"And just how do you figure that?" Satan asked.

"Well, I do keep population pressure off your place," God said, "and of course there's a certain amount of wear and tear from the clawing and scratching of your people."

"That's outrageous," the devil objected. "I won't pay a cent."

"Then I'll sue you," God threatened.

"Really?" The devil smiled. "Where will you find a lawyer?"

A man was sent to hell for his sins. As he was being taken to his place of eternal torment, he saw a lawyer making passionate love to a beautiful woman.

"What a ripoff," the man muttered. "I have to roast for all eternity, and that lawyer gets to spend it with a beautiful woman."

Jabbing the man with his pitchfork, his escorting demon snarled, "Who are you to question that woman's punishment?"

A lawyer was asked if he'd like to become a Jehovah's Witness.

He declined, as he hadn't seen the accident but would still be interested in taking the case.

A man walking down the street needs to know what two plus two equals.

Spotting a psychotherapist's office, he enters seeking the answer. The psychotherapist has him lie down on the couch and then tells him that perhaps, with a year of therapy, he can help him with his problem.

Dissatisfied, the man walks on until he comes to an engineer's office. The engineer starts furiously punching figures into his calculator. Eventually he says the answer is 3.9999 but he can round it out to four if he wants.

This still doesn't seem right, so he walks on until he comes to a lawyer's office. He is ushered in to see the lawyer and explains the problem. The lawyer thinks about it a minute, then puts his arm around the man's shoulders and asks, "What would you like it to be?"

Definition of *flagrant waste:*
A busload of lawyers going off the edge of a cliff, and there's one empty seat.

Three men—a doctor, a priest and a lawyer—go for a cruise on a power boat out of Miami. Suddenly the weather changes. The wind howls, waves are huge, and the boat is battered by heavy seas. Soon the radio breaks down, and the motor starts to fail.

Looking off the bow, one of the men spots an island about 150 yards away. "One of us will have to swim to that island for help," he says, and the others agree. To see who has to swim, they decide to draw straws.

The doctor draws the short straw, dives overboard, and about 50 yards from the boat is attacked by sharks. Blood stains the waves.

Again they draw straws and the priest gets the short end this time. Barely 25 yards from the boat, the sharks close in and tear him apart.

The storm intensifies and the boat starts to break up. The lawyer, now left alone, decides he'll risk the sharks to avoid drowning and leaps overboard. About 10 yards from the boat a giant white shark cruises up and says, "Climb on my back and I'll take you in."

After being deposited safely and gently on the shore, the lawyer is bewildered. "How come," he says, "you ate the doctor and the priest and not me?"

"Hey," grins the shark, "professional courtesy."

"Everyone in my family follows the medical profession," noted Smith. "They're lawyers."

Why does California have the most lawyers
and New Jersey the most toxic waste dumps?

New Jersey had first choice.

When we came to the court, there was the Lord Chancellor—the same whom I had seen in his private room in Lincoln's Inn—sitting in great state and gravity on the bench, with the mace and seals on a red table below him and an immense flat nosegay, like a little garden, which scented the whole court. Below the table, again, was a long row of solicitors, with bundles of papers on the matting at their feet; and then there were the gentlemen of the bar in wigs and gowns—some awake and some asleep, and one talking, and nobody paying much attention to what he said. The Lord Chancellor leaned back in his very easy chair with his elbow on the cushioned arm and his forehead resting on his hand; some of those who were present dozed; some read the newspapers; some walked about or whispered in groups: all seemed perfectly at their ease, by no means in a hurry, very unconcerned, and extremely comfortable.

To see everything going on so smoothly and to think of the roughness of the suitors' lives and deaths; to see all that full dress and ceremony and to think of the waste, and want, and beggared misery it represented; to consider that while the sickness of hope deferred was raging in so many hearts this polite show went calmly on from day to day, and year to year, in such good order and composure; to behold the Lord Chancellor and the whole array of practitioners under him looking at one another and at the spectators as if nobody had ever heard that all over England the name in which they were assembled was a bitter jest, was held in universal horror, contempt, and indignation, was known for something so flagrant and bad that little short of a miracle could bring any good out of it to any one—this was so curious and self-contradictory to me, who had no experience of it, that it was at first incredible, and I could not comprehend it.

from *Bleak House* by Charles Dickens — 1852

People who love sausage and respect the law should never watch either one being made.

The reason there's a penalty for laughing in court is that otherwise the jury would never be able to hear the evidence.

A jury is a collection of people gathered together to decide which side hired the better lawyer .

Applying for a job, the new lawyer was asked if paying back his law school tuition would be a problem.

"No," he replied. "I paid that back right after my first case."

"Really," said the interviewer. "What case was that?"

"Uh -- well, my dad sued me for it and won."

Q.

Do you know why medical testing laboratories now use lawyers instead of rats?

A.
Lawyers breed faster, so there are more of them.

B.
Lab personnel don't get as emotionally attached to the lawyers.

C.

Lawyers will do things rats won't do.

What do you need when you have three lawyers up to their necks in concrete?

More concrete.

THE VICAR AND THE FROG

"This is the true but lamentable story of a good, a holy, but truly unfortunate man and his incredible experiences on a summer night and morning. He was, and had been for the preceeding years, the vicar of a small parish in the village of Middle Wallop. His cherished wife of some 20 years had recently departed her corporeal envelope, leaving the vicar a very lonely man indeed.

"A year ago, on a summer night at dusk, the vicar was strolling, as had been his wont for some many years, in the woods near his beloved church. He was meditating on the relationship of man and his creator when he heard, 'Vicar! Vicar!'

"Although hearing the words, the vicar completely ignored them as being auricularly irrelevant since these woods had always been his sanctuary, quite unmolested by interlopers of any sort.

"But, shortly, 'Vicar! Vicar!'

"Finding it impossible to avoid this inter-ruption further, he turned to ascertain the identity of this incivility. There, at his feet, was a small green frog looking directly up at him, and, quite inescapedly, the origin of these bewildering words. Fully cognizant that the Almighty functioned in mysterious ways, he accepted this phenomenon and directly inquired, 'Who are you? What right have you to address me? A frog? This is preposterous!'

"But the diminutive amphibian was not to be rebuffed by this challenge. 'Vicar. Please listen. Hear my sad story and I know you won't reject my plea.'

" 'Get on with it, frog,' " said the exas-perated vicar. " 'Vicar, I have been the victim of a terrible and evil witch who cast a spell on me and transformed me from a simple and good choir boy living in the next village to this present form, a lowly frog. She did this merely to demonstrate her power over such as me, and there is only one way to undo this horrible act. You must help me, Vicar, because it is only you that can effect my release from this dreadful condition. My only hope is for you to let me spend one whole night in your bed, close to your goodness and holiness. That, if done, will break the spell and free me from the witch's influence. Please, please help me, Vicar. My life is in your hands.'

"Most reluctantly, the vicar acceded to this fervent, if odd, supplication. He escorted the frog, cupped securely in his hands, back to the vicarage, placed him beside him in his bed, and promptly fell off into a fitful sleep.

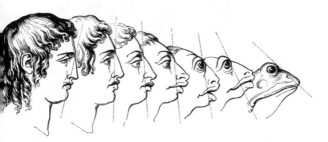

"At the breaking of the dawn the next morning the vicar turned over in his bed and saw there, lying snugly beside him, a blue-eyed, curly-locked choir boy deep in slumber. At this exact moment, the vicar's housemaid entered the bedroom with the vicar's morning tea."

"And that, my Lord, ladies and gentlemen of the jury, will be the case for the Defense."

One lawyer in a small town will starve to death, but two can make a pretty good living.

What's the difference between a lawyer and a rooster?

The rooster clucks defiance!

What's the difference between a porcupine and two lawyers in a Porsche?

With a porcupine, the pricks are on the outside.

According to lawyers, a bachelor is a selfish person who has cheated some deserving woman out of her divorce settlement.

Two cleaning ladies who work in a large law office building were talking one night.

"You know," one said to the other, "yesterday I asked an attorney on the third floor if I should wash his windows—and he billed me $65 for his time!"

roverbs

A peasant between two
lawyers is like a fish between
two cats.
 Spanish proverb
 H.L. Mencken, *A New Dictionary
 of Quotations,*
 1946

Ignorance of the law does
not prevent the losing lawyer
from collecting his bill.
 Anonymous
 Laurence J. Peter,
 Peter's Quotations, 1977

It's an ill cause that the
lawyer thinks shame o'.
 Scottish proverb
 H.L. Mencken, *A New Dictionary
 of Quotations,* 1946

"Virtue down the middle,"
said the Devil as he sat down
between two lawyers.
Danish proverb
H.L. Mencken, *A New Dictionary
of Quotations,* 1946

Winning a cat you lose a cow.
Chinese proverb
William Scarborough,
Chinese Proverbs, 1875

The worse the society, the
more law there will be. In Hell
there will be nothing but law
and due process will be meticu-
lously observed.
Grant Gilmore
New York Times, Feb. 23, 1977

No answer is a type
of answer.
Jewish folk saying
Joseph L. Baron, *A Treasury of
Jewish Quotations,* 1956

A piece of paper blown by
the wind into a law-court may
in the end only be drawn out
again by two oxen.
Chinese proverb
S.G. Champion, *Racial Proverbs,*
1938

Bad Jokes

•

My lawyer had a bad accident.

An ambulance backed over him.

•

Vacationing out west, the just divorced man stopped off in a bar. After a few drinks, he fell to thinking about his divorce, and thought out loud, "Lawyers are horses' asses." The bartender hustled over and said, "Mister, for God's sake—don't talk like that around here. Don't you know you're in horse country?"

•

How many legs does a sheep have if you call the tail a leg?

Well, five then.

No, four, because calling the tail a leg doesn't make it one.

•

Do you know why being a lawyer is the opposite of having sex?

Because it's all bad and some is worse.

Did you hear about the attorney who was a sports mechanic on the side?

He fixed basketball games.

•

The lawyer came home at 3 A.M. His wife hollored at him, "Where have you been, you cad? You said you'd be back at 11:45, and you're late!" "Nothing of the sort," said the lawyer. "I'm on time. I said I'd be back by a quarter of twelve."

•

Then there was the lawyer who, when he stepped in cow dung, thought he was melting.

•

What has four legs and chases cats?

Mrs. Katz and her lawyer.

•

There once was a lawyer
   named Rex
With a diminutive organ
   of sex
When charged with exposure
   he pleaded with composure
*De minimus non
   curat lex*

anyone can make up a joke better than the ones on the preceeding pages. Here's your chance:

Once upon a time _____

_____

_____

_____

_____

_____

Did you hear the one about _____

_____

_____

_____

_____

_____

_____

_____

_____

See, there was this travelling salesman who _____

_____

_____

_____

_____

_____

_____

_____

send new jokes to
SON OF SKID MARKS
Shelter Publications, Inc.
P.O. Box 279
Bolinas, CA 94924

The following joke is not about lawyers, but is often used by lawyers to illustrate the subtleties involved in some negotiations:

In the middle of the 19th Century, the Queen of England was visiting the continent and was traveling in her elegant carriage, with a retinue of persons of various importance following in a line of carriages behind her. As she came to a narrow bridge, which would not allow carriages to pass each other, her major-domo saw the Queen of Naples in an equally elaborate procession who was about to cross the bridge from the other side. It became immediately evident that one of the two Queens' processions was going to have to back up its carriages and horses, put them in the ditch, and make room for the other to pass. Obviously, the dignity and convenience of the Queens required that their major-domos try to arrange that his Queen be the one to cross the bridge, while the other procession backed into the ditch.

The major-domo of the Queen of England, who was elegantly attired in a velvet suit, wearing a plumed cap, climbed up on top of her carriage. With a deep bow and doffing the feathered headpiece in the direction of the Queen of Naples's procession, he announced in a loud voice as follows: "Here travels Her Majesty, the Queen of England, Sovereign of the Seven Seas, the Commander in Chief of the Royal Army and Navy, and the ruler of an empire upon which the sun never sets."

Not to be deterred, on the opposite end of the bridge, the major-domo of the Queen of Naples climbed to the top of her carriage. He was equally elegantly attired in a velvet suit with a plumed cap, and he bowed equally deeply while doffing his cap in the direction of the Queen of England, as he said: "What do you think I have here, a piece of shit?"

Acknowledgments

CREDITS

Publisher: Lloyd Kahn, Jr.
Editor: Michael Rafferty
Typesetting: Trudy Renggli
Book Design: Michael Rafferty & Lloyd Kahn, Jr.
Cover: David Wills
Hand Tinting: Sally Wetherby
Printing: Malloy Lithographing, Inc.,
              Ann Arbor, MI.
Type set on IBM Electronic Composer run by a
Pilara 2000 word processor.
Type is Press Roman.

ART CREDITS

Many of the illustrations are wood engravings done in
the late 19th century by anonymous American artists.

For other illustrations we are grateful to the following
artists: Thomas Nast, Pieter Brueghel, George
Cruikshank, *Punch,* G. Heck, Henry Winkler, William
Hogarth, Grandville and Michelangelo.

Art work on pp. 12, 56, 65 & 88 provided by
Bettmann Archive, New York, N.Y. Newspaper
clippings courtesy of San Francisco Chronicle, San
Francisco, Calif. Proverbs (pp. 84 and 85) reprinted
by permission from *The Quotable Lawyer,* edited by
David Schrager and Elizabeth Frost. (c) 1985, Facts
on File Inc., New York, N.Y.

Special thanks to Dover Publications, Inc., Varick,
N.Y., for preserving a great deal of early American art.

> The World has joked incessantly for over
> 50 centuries, and every joke that's possible
> has long ago been made.
> —Sir William Schwenk Gilbert, 1894

JOKE CREDITS

Upon soliciting jokes (via mail and newspaper ads)
we often received many versions of the same joke.
Credit, as listed below, goes to the person first
sending us the particular joke.

William M. Boulos .... p. 16
Phil Buchanan 12
Bill Bullis 87
Burr Carrington 87
Donald Casey 72
Lawrence W. Cohan 23
David Cole 70
Andy Crow 38
Charles Dickens 57
Dorinda Ennis 24
Peter Gubbins 75
Bruce Johnson 48
Bob Kahn 29
Abraham Lincoln 86
Pamela Jane Lewis 78
Bob Prichard 66
Adam Shawula 86
Dan Solo 18
Bruce Stilson, Bruce Bryson .... 8, 20, 26 & 90
Guy Stilson .... 14, 59, 76 & 82
James Targonsky 10, 30, 36, 43, 52, 60
.... 62, 64, 80 & 86
John van der Zee .... 41 & 86
Paul Wingate .... 50 & 54

2,026 Applicants Pass Bar Exam

By Michael Harris

Last December there was one lawyer for every 264 California residents. Now there is one for every 259.

The State Bar reported yesterday that 2,026 applicants passed February's State Bar examination, bringing the total number of lawyers eligible to practice in California to a record 105,437.

In 1960, the state got along with 19,355 lawyers, and in 1970 the total was 67,375.

The results of this winter's bar examinations showed a marked improvement over those since 1980. This year, 42.8 percent of the 4,734 applicants passed the three-day examination; last year's success rate was 28.4 percent.

The last time the February exam produced a better than 40 percent success rate was in 1979, when 43.9 percent of the applicants qualified to practice in California.

Results from the February tests are generally lower than those given in July, when many new law school graduates pass the bar on their first try. Slightly more than 70 percent of those who took the exam in February had also taken it last July and failed.

The State Bar reported that 52 percent of the applicants who attended American Bar Association-approved law schools passed February's bar exam — compared with 33.8 percent in February 1986.

A detailed analysis showing what law schools fared best in the exam is not yet completed, nor have the results been compiled by sex. An informal sample of the results indicates that slightly more than 40 percent of the successful applicants were women.

Students from schools that lacked the American Bar Association's imprimatur had a 35.1 passing rate — up from 23.4 percent last year.

As usual, the State Bar of California claimed the tests do not vary in difficulty from year to year. Students are required to complete multiple choice exams, write six essays and pass two performance tests designed to show their ability to combine legal knowledge with practical skills.

The new lawyers will be admitted to the bar in ceremonies that will begin June 17 in San Francisco, Los Angeles, Sacramento and other prominent centers of litigation. The oath-taking will conclude June 23 in Fresno.

"He who laughs, lasts."
    —Mary Pettibone Poole, 1938

THE TYRANTS FOE, THE PEOPLES FRIEND

Shelter Publications, Inc.,
P.O. Box 279
Bolinas, CA 94924